NUT-CRACKERS

S. I. F. F. B. R. H. B. B. O. T. H. B. A. B.
Santa is fighting fit H robin has
been bonked
on the head by
a babby.

1 2 3 4 5
2 3 4 5 6
3 4 5 6 7
4 5 6 7 8
5 6 7 8 9

JOHN JAWORSKI
and
IAN STEWART

NUT-CRACKERS

Puzzles and games to
boggle the mind

---

*Illustrated by
'Cosgrove' and Jozef Plojhar*

A Piccolo Original

PAN BOOKS LTD
LONDON

First published 1971 by Pan Books Ltd,
33 Tothill Street, London, S.W.1.

ISBN 0 330 02795 6

Made and printed in Great Britain by
Cox & Wyman Ltd, London, Reading and Fakenham

How to use this book

Within these pages you will find puzzles, games, magic tricks, things to do, things to make, things to look at . . . so there is no reason why you should read the pages in order. You can dip in wherever you like, and read what catches your eye. Occasionally, you may need to know something from an earlier section, but when this happens we have told you where to find it.

The answers to the puzzles are arranged in order at the back of the book, beginning on page 106.

We would like to thank (indeed, *do* thank!) 'Cosgrove' and Jozef Plojhar for drawing the diagrams; and Jim Bates, John Hart, and Robin Jones for many helpful ideas. The Professor Crankshaft cartoons are adapted from MANIFOLD and appear with the permission of MANIFOLD Publications, University of Warwick.

J.J.
I.N.S.

Royal Leamington Spa
August 1970

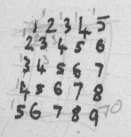

1 PROFESSOR CRANKSHAFT'S STAIRCASE

Our friend Professor Crankshaft is an inventor. Here he is at work in his laboratory.

We went over to see him the other week. As we approached his house we heard lots of bangs and thumps coming from it. We rang the doorbell three times before they stopped. After a short pause the Professor appeared at the door and let us in.

'Sorry to keep you waiting,' he said, 'but I didn't hear you. Someone making a noise somewhere. Let me show you my latest invention.'

We followed him down a passageway past a stuffed gorilla into a large workshop, full of tools and pieces of wood. He walked over to one peculiar object and patted it absently with his hand.

'This is it,' he said proudly.

We inspected it closely.

'Er . . . what is it?' we finally asked.

'Oh, sorry. I haven't quite finished it,' he replied.

Then he picked up some wood and a few nails and hammered loudly for ten minutes or so. When he had finished we looked again. His invention looked like this:

'A staircase?'

'Yes. But a very unusual kind. Observe that it is possible to walk round and round for ever, going upwards all the time. If you get tired, you can go the other way and walk *downwards* all the time. It's wonderful for getting your weight down.'

'But surely, Professor, you *can't* have a staircase which goes round and round for ever,' we said.

'That's what I thought,' he replied. 'But I was wrong. As you can see.' And he jumped up on to it and ran round once or twice, just to prove the point.

We still weren't convinced.

'Professor, a staircase like that is *impossible*.'

8

'Ah, yes,' said he, with a twinkle in his eye. 'But then, you must remember that I only invent impossible things.'

We pressed him to explain further.

'It's like this,' he went on. 'It is perfectly possible to *draw* objects which cannot actually exist, even though at first sight they look as if they can. A sort of optical illusion.'

We said we thought we understood. But we still didn't understand how he could run up and down his impossible staircase.

'Ah,' said he. 'It is easy to *draw* impossible objects. Only *I* know how to make them!'

2 POSTMAN'S WALK

Here is a plan of part of our town. Can our postman start out at the GPO, and deliver his letters to each house without wasting time by going down any street twice?

Take a pencil and try to draw a line from the GPO

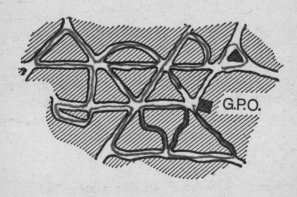

which goes along each street once and once only; it need not return to the GPO. There's a map to show you how in the back of the book, but try it yourself first.

3 THE MAGIC HONEYCOMB

You may have come across a *magic square*

$$8 \quad 1 \quad 6$$
$$3 \quad 5 \quad 7$$
$$4 \quad 9 \quad 2$$

in which all the lines of numbers (across, down, or diagonally) add up to 15. There are more complicated arrangements of numbers of the same type. In the following honeycomb arrangement any row of numbers, either across or diagonal, adds up to 38.

Can you find a way of arranging the numbers 1 to 16

in a four-by-four square so that each line across or down adds up to the same number? You will find one way of doing this in the answers at the back of the book.

4 CROSSNUMBER

A crossnumber is like a cross*word*, only using the numbers 0,1,2,3,4,5,6,7,8,9 instead of the letters of the alphabet. Here is one; all of the clues are about *time*.

Across:

(1) The number of days in a year.
(3) The number of minutes in a quarter of an hour.
(4) The number of seconds in one hour twenty-three minutes thirty-three seconds.
(6) The number of seconds in five minutes.
(7) The number of hours in a year.
(8) The number of hours in four days.
(10) The number of days in a leap year.

Down:

(1) The number of days in October.
(2) The number of seconds in an hour and a half.
(3) The number of hours in a week.
(4) The number of hours in twenty days twenty hours.
(5) The number of hours in a fortnight.
(6) The number of seconds in one hour three seconds.
(9) The number of hours in a day and a half.

You will find the answers at the back of the book. There will be more crossnumbers scattered through the book.

5 CHOP-STICK

So-called because you chop up a piece of paper and stick the bits together again. This is a very old Chinese puzzle. Take a square piece of cardboard and cut it into seven pieces like this:

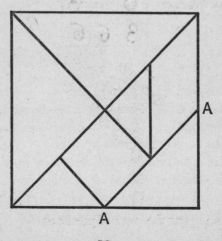

The points marked 'A' are in the middle of two sides. Having made a set of pieces, called *tans*, (after their inventor, the mythical T'an) you fit them together to make shapes (called *tangrams*): geometrical designs, people, animals, and so on. Here are some possibilities:

You can make up lots for yourself. If you keep a pencil and paper handy you can note down any that you like.

Now we'll give you a problem. How can you fit the seven *tans* together to get this stork?

The answer is at the back of the book.

6 COWS AND BULLS

This is a game for two people. One of you thinks of a four-figure number, like this: 1753, making sure that all the figures are different. It's as well to write this number down, so that no one can accuse you of changing it afterwards.

The other player than makes a four-figured guess at the number. He might say: 1234, for example.

The first player then tells him how many 'cows' and 'bulls' he has scored. A *cow* is a figure like the 3 that appears in both the number and the guess, but not in the right place. A *bull* is a figure that is in the number *and* in the correct place. '1' is a bull in the example above.

The second player has to guess the first player's number correctly after no more than *eight* guesses. Otherwise, the first player wins.

7 CURIOUS RINGS!

If we take two rings made of solid metal without any hidden catches or breaks, then you will agree that the rings must be either linked or unlinked.

If we take three rings, joined together like the ones below, things are not quite so simple. Look very closely at the diagram. Can you pull any of the rings away from the others? No, you can't: the three rings are linked together.

But suppose that one of the rings was removed (by magic perhaps!). Then the other two rings wouldn't be joined together at all! It doesn't matter which ring you choose to remove (in the diagram below we've removed them all, one at a time so that you can see for yourself). Whichever ring is removed, the other two fall apart. But with all three rings together, the rings are firmly linked.

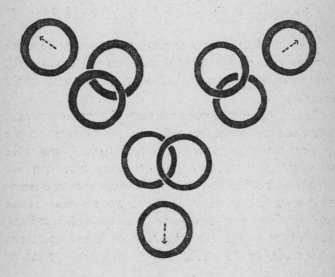

These rings are well known. They are part of the coat-of-arms of the Italian Borromeo family, and they are sometimes called the *Borromean Rings*. In America they have been used as the trademark of a brewery.

It is very easy to make a set of Borromean Rings from string, so that you can see for yourself that they really are linked together in this way.

8 A MATHEMATICAL WORD-GAME

If I write down the number ONE as a word, it has 3 letters, TWO has 3 letters, and so on. FOUR has 4 letters, and is the only number which has the same number of letters in its name as itself. However, there are lots of phrases that describe numbers; and some of these have the same number of letters as the number they describe: ONE-HALF OF THIRTY-SIX has 18 letters, and 18 is half of 36. TWELVE PLUS ONE has 13 letters.

There are lots of ways of playing this game. Here are two ways to play it by yourself; you can easily work out ways of playing it in competition with your friends.

First, try to find as many phrases like this as you can. You need not be too mathematical; if you lived on the number 41 bus route you might decide that THE NUMBER OF THE BUS THAT PASSES OUTSIDE MY HOUSE was a fair way to play. But you would have to be careful not to cheat. You can keep a note of the ones you find, and as you learn new ways of describing numbers at school, the list will grow. When you learn what a *cube* is you will be able to add TWO CUBED or 8 to your list.

The second way is to make a list of all the numbers from 1 to 100, or 200, or whatever you choose, and try to fill in against each number a way of describing it that has the correct number of letters. Of course, you will have trouble with the low numbers; we doubt that you will fill in many below 10.

If you get a long list with most of the numbers filled

in, we would be interested to see a copy of it. You can write to us c/o the publisher, whose address is at the front of this book. Happy hunting!

9 THE RIDDLE OF THE SPHINX

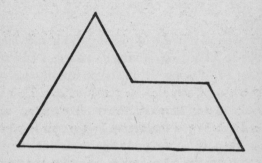

This shape is called a sphinx, because it looks a bit like a side view of the famous sphinx in Egypt. Can you fit four sphinxes together to make another sphinx, twice as large? You will find the answer at the back of the book. One way to try it is to cut out four sphinxes from cardboard (trace the diagram using tracing paper) and see if you can fit them together.

This is a trick for guessing a number.

Ask someone to think of a number, less than 10. Tell him to add 1, double the result, multiply by 5, substract 3, multiply by 5 again, subtract 8, double the answer, and add 7. Ask him what the result is. At once you tell him the original number that he thought of.

Method: his result will be a number ending in 61. *If it isn't you tell him he has made a mistake*, which is an even better trick! Knock off these two figures, and you will be left with the answer.

As an example, suppose he starts with 7. He obtains successively these numbers: $7+1 = 8$, $8 \times 2 = 16$, $16 \times 5 = 80$, $80-3 = 77$, $77 \times 5 = 385$, $385-8 = 377$, $377 \times 2 = 754$, $754+7 = 761$.

Knocking off the 61 we get 7, the number he chose to start with.

It *always* works, even with numbers *over* 10! But you will need pencil and paper to work the numbers out, unless you are *very* good at mental arithmetic.

11 PROFESSOR CRANKSHAFT'S BOOKCASE

Even when Professor Crankshaft tries something simple, like making a bookcase, he still ends up with an impossible result!

12 WHAT'S NEXT?

You've seen this sort of puzzle before. Which is the next number in each of the sequences below?

(a) 1, 3, 5, 7, 9, 11, ?

(b) 1, 4, 9, 16, 25, ?

(c) 1, 2, 4, 8, 16, 32, ?

(d) 1, 2, 4, 7, 11, 16, ?

(e) 1, 1, 2, 3, 5, 8, 13, ?

The answers are at the back of the book.

13 HUGS AND KISSES

When this game was invented, it wasn't called 'Hugs and Kisses'. It was called 'Gale' after the man who invented it, a professor of economics in an American university. 'Hugs and Kisses' sound a rather more interesting name, though!

You need to draw the board with hugs (o) and kisses (x) like this:

One player is the hugs and one is the kisses. You need a pencil. The hugs-player goes first (hugs are always before kisses!) and joins together any two neighbouring hugs by a straight line. Then the kisses-player joins any two kisses together, and so on. The lines must not cross. The winner is the player who first makes an unbroken line joining the opposite sides of the board. The hugs-player must get a line across the board from left to right and the kisses-player must get a line from top to bottom. The winning line will probably snake all over the board. A game that is part-played already is this one:

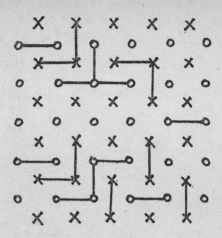

There can't ever be a draw, because the only way that hugs can stop the kisses winning is to win himself. The only sure way of stopping someone getting a line across the page is to draw a line down the page. Here is a game that has ended in a win for the kisses:

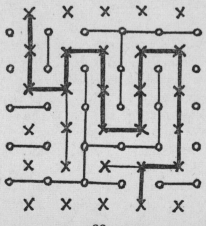

14 TANGRAMS

Can you make these shapes using the seven *tans*? (See page 12.)

Answers are at the back of the book.

15 SKELETONS

Here is part of a crossword:

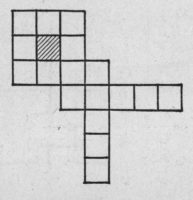

The idea of the puzzle is to fill it in, *using only the names of numbers*, like ONE, TWO, SEVENTEEN, and so on. The skeleton above can be filled in like this:

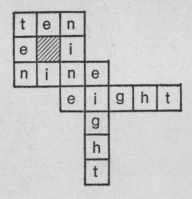

Can you fill in the next two skeletons with number-names? You will find the answers at the back of the book.

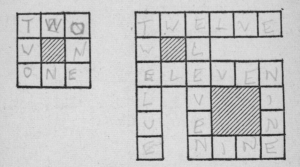

16 FALSEHOODS

Exactly one of these numbered statements is true.

(1) One of these statements is false.
(2) Two of these statements are false.
(3) Three of these statements are false.
(4) Four of these statements are false.
(5) Five of these statements are false.

   Which is the true statement? You will find the answer at the back of the book.

17 LONG MULTIPLICATION

NOT the usual sort of long multiplication!
   Suppose you have a sheet of paper one sixteenth of an inch thick and fold it in half ten times. How thick will it be then? Before reading on, take a sheet of newspaper and see how many times you can fold it in half. Did you get to ten? No, you didn't. After about eight folds you had a thick wad of paper, and it was too stiff to fold again. You now won't be quite so surprised to learn that the answer to the question is:

Five feet four inches!

   How do we work this out? Each time you fold the paper you double the thickness. So:

One fold multiplies by   2
Two folds multiply by twice 2 which is   ..   4

3 folds multiply by twice 4 which is	..	8
4 folds multiply by twice 8 which is	..	16
5 folds multiply by twice 16 which is	..	32
6 folds multiply by twice 32 which is	..	64
7 folds multiply by twice 64 which is	..	128
8 folds multiply by twice 128 which is	..	256
9 folds multiply by twice 256 which is	..	512
10 folds multiply by twice 512 which is	..	1024

So folding 10 times multiplies the thickness by 1024, giving $\frac{1}{16} \times 1024 = 64$ inches, or 5 feet 4 inches.

If you continue doubling, the numbers get very large indeed. If you fold the paper 100 times its thickness is multiplied by:

$$1267650600228229401496703205376$$

or rather more than a million million million million million!

18 SEAMUS ANDROID

This game is like tangrams (see *Chop-stick*, page 12). Cut out a set of pieces from card, like this:

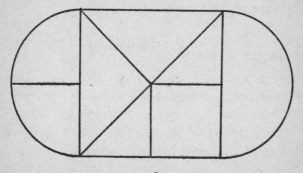

Now see what shapes you can make with them. We named the game after our cat because the first two shapes we made looked like him:

Can you work out how the pieces fit to make these two pictures of Seamus Android? You will find the answers at the back of the book, and there will be some more Seamus Android puzzles scattered through the rest of the book.

You can also try to make up new shapes of your own.

19 SPROUTS

This is a pencil-and-paper game for two players, invented by John Conway, a lecturer at Cambridge University. You start by drawing four or five dots at random as on the next page.

And then follow these rules:

Rule 1 Players play alternately.

Rule 2 You play by joining two dots with a line (curved or straight; you can make it as wiggly as you like as long as it doesn't cross itself) and then drawing a new dot in the middle of your line. Like this:

● ● becomes

Rule 3 Lines may not cross each other or pass through dots (except the new dot in the middle!).

Rule 4 No dot may have more than three lines coming from it, like this:

Rule 5 The first player who cannot move *loses*.

28

To help you get the idea, we give an example of a complete game, move by move:

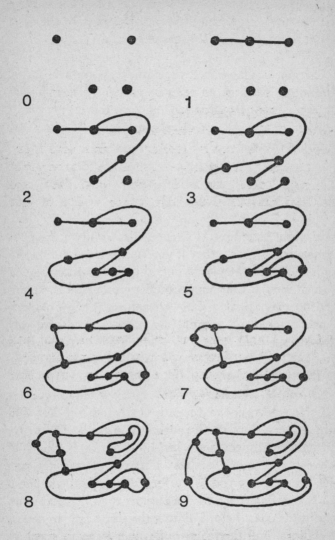

In the last diagram (number 9) the second player cannot move. Although there are dots with fewer than three lines coming out of them, he cannot join them with a new line because the old lines get in the way. The first player wins this game.

Sprouts can be played very quickly, produces lots of interesting patterns, and can be varied by starting with different numbers of dots. Don't use more than about six dots or the game will take too long. It can never end in a draw.

20 MONKEY-PUZZLE

You might have heard someone say – or if you haven't, I'm saying it now – that if you had a large number of monkeys sitting at a large number of typewriters, given a long enough time they would type out all the plays and poems of Shakespeare. Of course, they would also type out a lot of meaningless rubbish (and probably this whole book too). The whole idea is that if a monkey types letters one after another at random, some of the time the letters make words by pure chance.

Of course, the chance that a monkey might type out all the works of Shakespeare correct to the last full-stop is very, very small indeed. You might like to try a small experiment to see just how small this chance is. Take two dice and a sheet of paper. Throw the first die (*die* is the correct word for just one of them, *dice* is for two or more) and look along the row with that number in the chart below. Throw the second die to choose a column, and then find out which letter or space or comma or whatever your monkey has 'typed'. If you don't get a sensible word to begin with, start again.

		second die					
		1	2	3	4	5	6
	1	A	B	C	D	E	F
	2	G	H	I	J	K	L
first	3	M	N	O	P	Q	R	*means
die	4	S	T	U	V	W	X	a space
	5	Y	Z	.	,	!	?
	6	*	*	*	*	*	*

How many times did you have to try before you got a sensible word? If you get your 'monkey' to type out lots and lots of three-letter words, how many of them made sense?

Guess how long it would probably take 100 monkeys, working at one letter a second, to type out the words 'Dear Sir'. When you've made a guess, look at the answers in the back of the book to see how near you were!

21 THE CRANKSHAFT LECTURES

Professor Crankshaft was recently invited to give a lecture to the Society for the Abolition of Dinosaurs, but when he tried to clean the blackboard he got carried away . . . (See over page.)

22 WHAT TO DO WHEN YOU'VE GOT YOURSELF LOST IN A MAZE

If you've visited Hampton Court Palace, outside London, you've probably seen the maze that they have there. It's one of the few mazes left nowadays that you can actually walk round, although a hundred years ago they were very popular. You will certainly have seen some mazes in puzzle books like this one, or in newspapers. *In all these mazes the object is to find a path from the entrance to the centre* (or sometimes from one point in the maze to another point).

This section is a little bit longer than most others in the book, because mazes are interesting and we thought you might like to learn something about them. Some people know some half-truths about mazes, and those can lead them into as much trouble as knowing nothing at all!

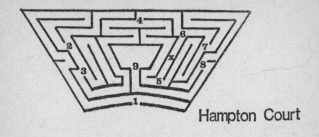

Hampton Court

For example: a lot of people think that if you are lost in a maze you should put your hand on to the right-hand wall and keep following the wall, never removing your hand; and this will take you back to the entrance. This is only a half-truth; if you were lost in Hampton Court maze at the spot marked X and tried this method, you would just go round and round in circles; if you switched hands and used the left-hand wall you wouldn't do much better! You'd get very tired and hungry and wish you knew *more* about mazes!

The main point about mazes is that they are not really as complicated as they look. There are lots of corners and twists and turns, but at most corners you can only turn *one way*. The only thing that you have to worry about in a maze is what to do at a *junction*; which direction do you take? And, provided you have lots of time, it doesn't really matter how far you walk in between junctions. So we could draw a diagram which irons out the twists and turns, like the London Transport Underground railway map, which shows only the important things like stations and where the lines cross. To make a simpler map of Hampton Court maze, we could draw one like this:

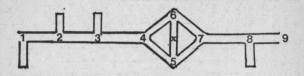

and if we took this map with us in the maze we could easily find our way through it.

Of course, you may not believe us when we say that this map is the same as Hampton Court maze. But you can always check it – it's always a good idea to check anything you aren't sure of: however careful we are, we may have made a mistake. We've numbered the junctions on both plans to help you. Thus, if we are at junction 8, coming from 7, we have two choices: turn right, which leads to a dead end, or go straight on which gets us to the centre (after a little twisting and turning). From the simple diagram it is easy to see what goes wrong with the 'hand-on-wall' method; you could very easily go round the 4-5-6 loop or the 5-6-7 loop for ever!

It is always much easier to solve a maze problem if we have a plan of the maze because we can see all the bits at once. It's harder if we are actually *inside* the maze! With a map, we can shade in all the dead ends, which usually leaves a much simpler maze to solve. If we start with this maze:

(which is another famous one that used to be in the grounds of Hatfield House in Hertfordshire) and shade in dead ends we get this:

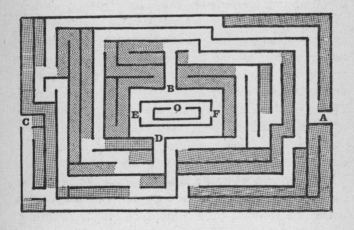

and we can draw a simplified London Underground type map of it easily, as shown on the next page.

This shows that it is really very easy to get from the entrance to the centre. But it you are at the centre and use the 'hand-on-wall' method, you'll never get out! You'd go round and round one of the loops centre-E-D-F or centre-E-F. And if you started at an entrance and put your hand on the wall you'd get to the *other* entrance, but miss the centre completely! In fact, if you start with your hand on a wall at the entrance you will always get back to an entrance. *So, if you want to have a walk through a maze without getting lost, put your hand on the wall and keep it there from the very beginning.* But if you do this you may not reach the centre.

In the rest of the book we've slipped in a few mazes as the mood took us. There isn't any need to give answers because you can always turn back to this section and use one of the methods we've given here. Good luck!

23 SHORTHAND CROSSNUMBER

Mathematicians sometimes use a shorthand for writing numbers like $3 \times 3 \times 3 \times 3 \times 3$. This has 5 threes multiplied together, and is written 3^5. The bottom number is the one you use; the top one tells you how many to multiply together. So $11^2 = 11 \times 11 = 121$, $5^3 = 5 \times 5 \times 5 = 125$. Here is a crossnumber with all the clues in 'shorthand':

1	▧	2	3	
4	5			▧
6		▧	7	8
▧	9	10		
11			▧	

Across:

  (2) 19^2

  (4) 12^3

  (6) 3^3

  (7) 3^4

  (9) 86^2

(11) 31^2

Down:

  (1) 2^9

  (2) 2^5

  (3) 83^2

  (5) 6^5

  (8) 13^2

(10) 31^1

The answer is at the back of the book.

24 REP-TILES

That is, TILES which REPeat their shape (or REP-licate). Can you fit four of these shapes together to make one the same shape but twice as big? You can either draw them or cut them out from card, copying this diagram:

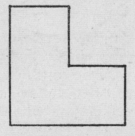

The answer is at the back of the book.

$$6 \times 6 = 36$$
$$66 \times 66 = 4356$$
$$666 \times 666 = 443556$$
$$6666 \times 6666 = 44435556$$
$$66666 \times 66666 = 4444355556$$
$$666666 \times 666666 = 444443555556$$
$$6666666 \times 6666666 = 44444435555556$$
$$66666666 \times 66666666 = 4444444355555556$$
$$666666666 \times 666666666 = 444444443555555556$$

Can you guess what $6666666666 \times 6666666666$ is? The answer is at the back of the book.

26 CRANKSHAFT THE ILLUSIONIST

'I was talking about optical illusions,' said Professor Crankshaft suddenly.

Before we could say anything he picked up a piece of paper and drew rapidly these sketches:

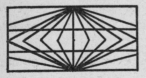 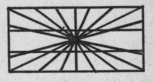

'You see how the horizontal lines curve,' he went on. 'One pair curve inwards, one outwards.'

'Yes.'

'Well, actually, all the lines are perfectly straight.

No bends at all. You can check with a ruler if you don't believe me.'

We did, and he was right!

'The eye is fooled into thinking they are bent by the other lines in the diagram,' he said. 'Here's another one:

'Which has largest area, the black dot or the black ring?'

We thought it was the dot, but we were wrong. The correct answer is at the back of the book.

'Talking of blackness,' said the Professor, 'I have just invented an electric *dark* bulb. There it is, hanging from the ceiling.'

It looked exactly like an ordinary electric *light* bulb to us (it was even shining brightly) and we said so.

'Ah,' replied the Professor. 'It's not switched on yet.' He reached behind him and pressed a switch. At once the room plunged into darkness.

'Marvellous, isn't it?' came a voice through the blackness.

Here is a trick you can do using a calendar – preferably an old one!

While your back is turned a spectator selects a month of the calendar and draws a square round 9 dates (3 across by 3 down). Like this:

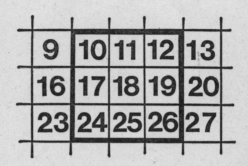

Now ask him to add up the 9 numbers inside the square; he will probably need a pencil and a sheet of paper!

You now announce that you have remarkable mathematical powers, and can perform long calculations very rapidly. Ask him for the smallest number in the three-by-three square (in this case he tells you the number 10). Almost immediately you tell him the sum of the nine numbers.

Method: add 8 to the number he gives you and multiply the result by 9.

For example, in the above he tells you 10. $10 + 8 = 18$, and $18 \times 9 = 162$. And $10 + 11 + 12 + 17 + 18 + 19 + 24 + 25 + 26 = 162$.

It's blackberry time, and along all the country lanes the blackberry bushes are weighed down with succulent fruit. Not wishing to waste time, you want to tour all the lanes picking berries, without going down any lane more than once, starting and finishing at your house (the black dot). How can you do this?

One method is shown at the back of the book; but you may find others. See how many different routes you can find!

29 SEAMUS ANDROID

Can you make these shapes using the set of Seamus Android pieces? (See page 26.)

The answers are at the back of the book.

30 HOW MANY?

How many squares can you count in this diagram? Be careful; some of the squares are parts of other squares.

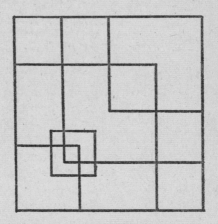

You will find the answer at the back of the book.

Take a strip of paper about two feet long and two inches broad. Newspaper will do, or brown wrapping paper. Join the ends with sticky tape or glue to form a closed band:

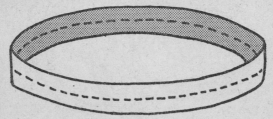

This band has two sides and two edges. If you cut it *lengthwise* down the middle (along the dotted line in the diagram), it falls into two pieces, each like the original band, but narrower. So far, nothing very interesting.

Now take another strip of paper, the same size; *twist it* once and join the ends, like this:

This band has only one side! If you don't believe me, try painting one side red. As you work round, because of the twist, you'll end up by covering the entire strip with red paint. It also has only one edge. Now cut it lengthwise down the middle, like the other band. You'd expect it to fall into two pieces, but it doesn't! Instead it forms a single loop, twice as long as the original one. Why?

Next make a loop with *two* twists. How many sides does it have? How many edges? If you cut it down the middle, you get two bands . . . but they are interlocked, like the links of a chain:

Most people are very surprised the first time they come across these funny strips. You can use them for a trick which is great fun at parties, or for amusing your friends. First, you must prepare three enormous strips of paper, about twelve feet long and eight inches wide. (The best way is to cut several strips of newspaper and join them end to end; or you may be lucky enough to have an old roll of wallpaper.) Make one band with one twist, one with two twists, and one with three twists. You pick up the band with no twists and announce that you are going to have a race. Each competitor will have a paper band and a pair of scissors, and the first person to cut his band down the middle *into two separate strips* will win a prize. You demonstrate this by cutting your band into two, getting two separate strips. Now you select two people from the audience, give them each a strip of paper (twisted!) and a pair of scissors. When you give the word they both begin madly cutting along the middle of their paper bands, *which is so large that they don't notice the twists*. (It probably wouldn't matter if

44

they did!) One of them finishes and rushes up carrying a pile of paper. Suppose it is the one who had the strip with one twist. You congratulate him on winning, and are just about to hand him the prize when you say 'Oh, we'd better check you've done it properly'. Imagine everyone's surprise when it turns out that all he has done is to produce a single strip twenty-four feet long! So you say 'Sorry, but you must have made a mistake somewhere' and go to give the prize to the other player. But his two loops are linked together, so they don't count as two separate pieces. This leads to a general collapse of the audience, and two very baffled competitors.

These twisted bands are often called Möbius Bands, in honour of the German mathematician who invented them. There are lots of other things you can do with them. Here are a few questions for you to answer:

(1) What happens if you cut a band with *three* twists? Try to guess first, then make one and see.

(2) What about four, five . . . twists? (You may have to use longer strips of paper.)

(3) What happens if you cut a one-twist band one-third of the way across, instead of down the middle, like this:

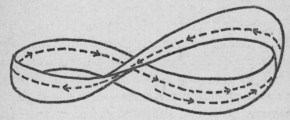

(4) Does what happens when you cut depend on the size of the bands, or only on the number of twists? (The answers are at the back of the book.)

This crossnumber goes in *three* directions:

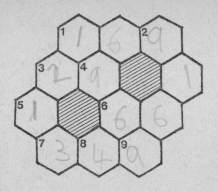

Across (→):
(1) 5 down multiplied by itself.
(3) 1 fewer than 2½ dozen.
(6) The largest 2-figure number turned upside down.
(7) The number of days in a year less the number of ounces in a pound.

Up (↗):
(4) 12 × 8.
(5) A century plus a score plus one.
(8) XLVI.
(9) 1 across backwards.

Down (↘):
(1) Year when Man first landed on the moon.
(2) Number of days in 13 weeks.
(5) A baker's dozen.

The answers can be found at the back of the book.

In this diagram there are three circles, each with four numbers written on it:

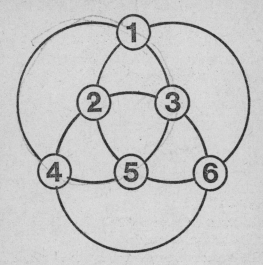

Curiously, the numbers on each circle add up to the same thing: 14.

Can you put the numbers 1, 2, 3, 4, 5, 6, into the spaces on this diagram:

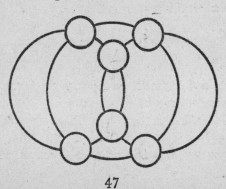

so that, again, the sum of the numbers on any circle is 14? You will find the answer at the back of the book.

34 PROFESSOR CRANKSHAFT'S WATERWHEEL

'The trouble with *ordinary* waterwheels,' said Professor Crankshaft one day, 'is that they use so much water. Now, what I propose is this.' And he drew the following sketch:

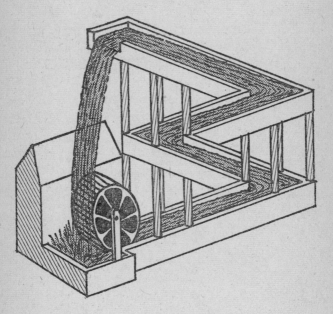

'You will observe,' he said, 'that the water flows in an endless loop, and none is wasted. You could fit an electrical generator to the wheel, and save electrical bills too!'

He paused.

'I could even connect it to my electric dark bulb . . .'

35 THINK OF A NUMBER

This is a magical trick for guessing *two* numbers at
once! Tell someone to select two numbers between 1
and 9. Ask him to multiply one of the numbers by 5,
add 7, double the sum, and add the other number.
When he tells you the result you tell him what the two
numbers were.

Method: subtract 14 from the result he tells you.
This will give a two-figure number. The two digits of
this number are the two numbers he started with.

As an example, suppose he starts with 6 and 8. He
multiplies 6 by 5, gets 30; adds 7, getting 37; doubles,
getting 74; and adds 8, giving a final result of 82. This is
the number he tells you. You subtract 14 from 82, getting 68. The two digits of this, 6 and 8, are the numbers
he started with.

Try this trick out on your friends, and see how long it
takes them to work out how you do it.

36 REVERSALS

Can you find:

(a) A two-figure number which has its digits reversed
    when 9 is added to it.
(b) A four-figure number which has its digits reversed
    when you *multiply* it by 9.

(c) A two-figure number which has its digits reversed
   when you double it and add 2.
(d) A two-figure number which has its digits reversed
   when you double it and subtract 1.

Answers are at the back of the book.

37 SIM

Sim (short for SIMple SIMmons, after its inventor,
Gustavus J. Simmons) is a game for two players. Start by
drawing six small circles on a piece of paper, like this:

Each player has a coloured pencil (say red and blue).
Players take turns to draw straight lines between any
two of the six small circles. The first player to form a
triangle with its corners on the circles *loses*. Here is a
sample game. We have shown the red lines as solid
lines and the blue lines as dotted lines; the moves are
numbered in the order of play.

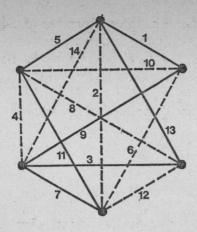

When red plays now he forms a triangle and loses.

This game cannot end in a draw, for which reason it is better than noughts and crosses. It is very suitable for playing on buses or trains.

38 MONEY PUZZLE

Take five coins of the same value. Can you place them so that each touches the other four? You will find the answer at the back of the book.

39 TOUR OF BRITAIN

On the map on the next page can you show how to get from John o'Groats to Land's End without crossing the solid lines?

John o'Groats

Land's End

40 CARDS THAT UNSHUFFLE THEMSELVES

Here is how to make a pack of cards that you can shuffle into any order that you like, so that they are completely mixed-up, and then unshuffle them in just four moves, which you can even learn to do with your eyes shut!

You will need 8 cards the same size; if you can get

hold of some cards about 3 inches by 5 inches used in card-index filing systems these are the best, but you can easily cut 8 cards of about the right size from stiff cardboard.

You will need to make holes in the cards exactly as shown in the picture on this page. It is very important that the holes are large and that they come in the same place on each card. You must measure carefully to make sure.

When you have cut out the holes and the slots, and numbered your cards, rearrange them into any order

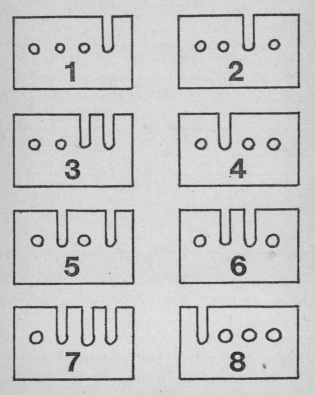

you like. Take a knitting needle, or a pencil – anything that will fit through your holes – and put it through the hole on the *right* of the pack of cards.

Then if you lift the needle up carefully, joggling it a little so that no cards get stuck, the cards with slots will fall away and those with holes will rise with the needle. Make sure that you don't change the order of them, and bring the cards of the needle to the front of the pack.

Now put your needle through the second hole from the right and repeat the process, then the third hole, then the last one – four times in all. You will find that the eight cards have rearranged themselves in the order 1 to 8.

Whatever order you put the cards into, you can always unshuffle them in four moves.

If you wanted to, you could also make a card numbered 0 which would have four holes but no slots cut out.

You can make a larger set of cards if you wish: to make a set up to number 15 you will need 7 more cards looking like the 1–7 cards you have already made, but with a slot instead of a hole at the left.

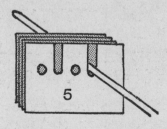

How are you going to number this set? There's a quick way given in the answers, if you can't think how.

41 SKELETONS

Here is another skeleton puzzle:

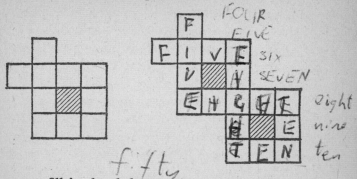

Can you fill in the skeletons with names of numbers?
(See page 23.) You will find the answers at the back of
the book.

42 CRANKSHAFT ON CODES

'When I make my best inventions,' said Professor
Crankshaft, 'I naturally want to write down the details.
But then somebody might steal the idea. So I use a
code. The simplest one I use is very straightforward,
just a substitution of one letter for another. I write out
two alphabets:

ABCDEFGHIJKLMNOPQRSTUVWXYZ
CRANKSHFTBDEGIJLMOPQUVWXYZ

And instead of the letters in the top row I use the ones
below them in the second row. Suppose I want to
write this message in code:

Your dinner is in the oven

'Underneath Y is the letter Y, under O is J, under U U, under R O, and so on ... I get the message:

YJUO NTIIKO TP TI QFK JVKI

'To decode, I work the other way: I replace each letter by the one above it, to get the original message.'

Now, suppose Professor Crankshaft writes this code message:

[handwritten: IF YOU CANT DECODE THIS MESSAGE]
TS YJU ACIO NKAJNK QFTP GKPPCHK
[handwritten: YOU WILL FIND THE]
YJU WTEE STIN QFK CIPWKO CQ QFK RCAD
JS QFK RJJD
[handwritten: ATSWER AT THE BACK OF THE BOOK]

What does it mean?

If you can't decode the message you will find the answer at the back of the book.

'Notice,' said the Professor, 'how easy it is to re-member the second alphabet. If you take the *keyword* CRANKSHAFT and write the letters of that first (omitting the second A) and then put in all the missing letters in order, you get the bottom line of the code.

'Of course, you can use other keywords if you like.'

43 LITTLE-UNS AND BIG-UNS

Make these shapes from cardboard (all the dotted squares are the same size. You could use squared paper if you wished). There are four puzzles in one.

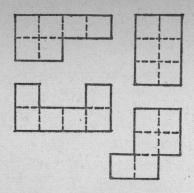

Select any one of the four shapes (say, the rectangle). Try to fit your four pieces together to make this shape, but twice as large.

Do this for each of the four shapes.

The answers are at the back of the book.

44 NUMBER PATTERNS

$$(8 \times 8) + 13 = 77$$
$$(88 \times 8) + 13 = 717$$
$$(888 \times 8) + 13 = 7117$$
$$(8888 \times 8) + 13 = 71117$$
$$(88888 \times 8) + 13 = 711117$$
$$(888888 \times 8) + 13 = 7111117$$
$$(8888888 \times 8) + 13 = 71111117$$
$$(88888888 \times 8) + 13 = 711111117$$
$$(888888888 \times 8) + 13 = 7111111117$$

Can you guess what $(8888888888 \times 8) + 13$ is? The answer is at the back of the book.

Read that title again *very* carefully indeed! This is a pencil-and-paper game that has nothing at all to do with any games that you might think it could be connected with.

To play Snakes-and-Adders you need to draw yourself a diagram like the one below. If you want, you can make a larger one with more squares, but if you have something smaller the game will probably be over too quickly.

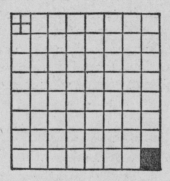

Two people are best to play this game, although you can play it with three. If there are four of you, it's best to play two separate games.

The first player starts in one of the squares next to the + sign and marks one of the following shapes in the squares:

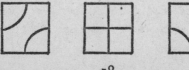

The second player must make one of the same three shapes, but he must make his mark in a square that carries on the wriggling line started by the first player. Like this:

After some while, you have a wriggling snake stretching round the paper. When you come to join up to a part of the snake that you have already drawn, but have not used yet, the part just becomes the next piece of snake. Sometimes the snake will cross itself, and when it does you just carry on from the other side, like this:

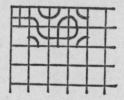

The first player who causes the snake to touch the edge of the diagram, or the shaded square at the bottom, is the loser. If you are playing with three people, this means that you have two winners which is why it is a better game for two people than for three. Here are the last few moves of a game, to show you how careful you must be when there are a lot of squares already filled in.

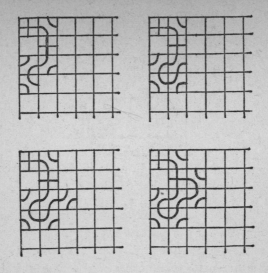

The last move of all is a particularly clever one. Whichever shape the other player makes on the next move, it will lead to the edge, either directly or indirectly. The player making the last move in the picture has won.

46 PROFESSOR CRANKSHAFT'S CHRISTMAS PRESENT

Professor Crankshaft's warped imagination is matched by his warm heart. Last Christmas he sent us a present. It came in a box like this:

We had some difficulty in opening it, and when we did we found these peculiar objects:

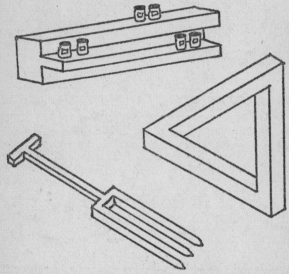

The first one, we discovered, was useful for shelving; we have drawn it with some jam-jars on it. But we couldn't work out what the other two were, so we asked the Professor. He said the fork was a garden fork for self-raising flowers. The triangle? That was 'Just a triangle. Thought it might come in useful for something.'

(It is, of course, an impossible triangle. The Professor made it out of impossible wood, just in case.)

47 TANGRAMS

Can you make these shapes using the seven *tans*? (See page 12).

Answers are at the back of the book.

48 WHAT'S NEXT?

These puzzles are *different*: that is to say, each of these number sequences is concerned with the *difference* between the numbers. What is the next number in each case?

(a) 1, 3, 6, 10, 15, ? 2¹
(b) 2, 3, 6, 11, 18, 27, ?
(c) 1, 3, 6, 12, 23, 41, ?
(d) 1, 3, 9, 27, 81, 243, ?
(e) 72, 81, 11, 6, 3, ?

The answers are at the back of the book.

49 APRIL FOOL QUIZ

All of these are trick questions, so be careful!

(1) How many grooves does a gramophone record have? 1

(2) How many months have 28 days? 1

(3) What word is always pronounced wrongly? *wrongly?*

(4) If I have 144 chickens and take away all but 10 how many do I have left? 10

(5) Which has more tails, one cat or no cat? 1

(6) What is at the middle of Paris? r

(7) What do you get if you add 1 to 16 four times?

(8) In how many years during a century do Christmas Day and New Year's Day fall in the same year? 100

(9) Can you build a house with all four sides facing North? Yes

(10) I have two coins in my pocket, together they add up to 55 new pence. One of them is not a 50-penny piece. What are they? 50p and 5p

See the back of the book for the answers.

50 GET KNOTTED!

This puzzle can be *very* puzzling indeed. You will need two pieces of string or rope about 2 feet or 3 feet long. Your mother will probably be very cross if you use your school tie for this trick, but it *is* just about the right length.

Tie the string across from one wrist to the other. Then get a friend to tie the other piece of string between his wrists, making sure that he is joined to you. This can be quite difficult, and having a third person around to do the tying is very useful. When you have finished, your hands should look like the picture on the next page.

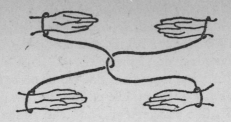

The puzzle is just this: get out! You and your friend must try to get apart without untying the knots and without breaking or cutting the string (which is doubly important if you *are* using your tie). If you can't get out, the solution is at the back of the book. We hope you can turn the pages of this book with your hands tied!

51 CRANKSHAFT IN PERSPECTIVE

'The eye,' said Professor Crankshaft, 'is a very curious instrument. It can see extremely fine details, and yet be misled by simple tricks. Like these two lines.

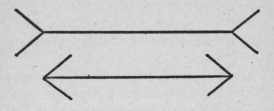

It looks as if the top line is longer than the other one, but in fact they are exactly the same length. It is the same in this diagram:

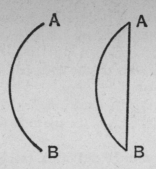

The points A, B are exactly the same distance apart in each case. And in this diagram:

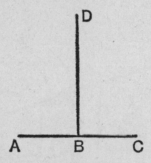

the distance AC is the same as BD.'

We listened, awestruck.

'The eye can be deceived in other ways,' he continued. 'In this diagram:

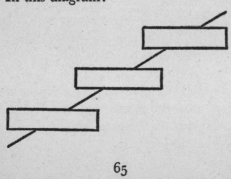

the lines between the blocks are actually part of the same straight line, but they look as if they are parts of *different* lines.'

We placed a ruler on the lines, and discovered that he was quite correct.

'I have developed a machine,' said the Professor, 'which uses this ability of the eye to be fooled. It makes things bigger.'

He stepped into the end of the machine and began to walk along it.

And as he walked he seemed to get bigger and bigger and bigger. But on measuring, we found that he always stayed exactly the same height.

How *does* he do it?

52 SEAMUS ANDROID'S VALENTINE

Can you make this heart shape from the Seamus Android pieces? (See page 26.)

Answers are at the back of the book.

53 STRANGE NUMBERS

A number multiplied by itself three times is called a *cube*, so that two cubed is $2 \times 2 \times 2 = 8$ (and using our 'shorthand' of page 36 we can write this as 2^3). There are exactly four three-figure numbers which are the sum of the cubes of their digits. They are:

$$153 = 1^3 + 5^3 + 3^3 = 1 + 125 + 27$$
$$370 = 3^3 + 7^3 + 0^3 = 27 + 343 + 0$$
$$371 = 3^3 + 7^3 + 1^3 = 27 + 343 + 1$$
$$407 = 4^3 + 0^3 + 7^3 = 64 + 0 + 343$$

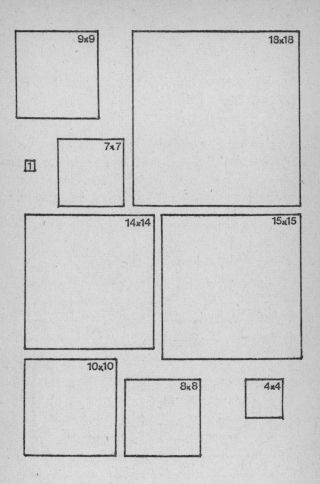

Here are nine squares of different sizes. Can you fit these squares together to make a rectangle that measures 32 squares by 33 squares? It's best to cut out a set of

squares from squared paper. To help we have given
their measurements, in units of a square.

The answer is at the back of the book.

55 A MAZE FOR PEOPLE WHO DON'T LIKE MAZES

This was a maze invented by two men called London
and Wise, who also designed Hampton Court maze.
If you use the methods of solving mazes that we've
described before (see page 32), you'll begin to wonder
why they bothered!

Can you set out from the arrow and get to the dot by
going along the paths in the maze?

Half full = half empty
Therefore . . .
full = empty!

57 REP-TILES

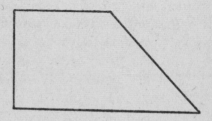

Can you fit nine pieces like this together to make a larger one which is the same shape but three times as big?

The answer is at the back of the book.

58 TOPSY-TURVY

Some numbers look the same when turned upside-down, like 0,1,8. Others look like different numbers when you turn them upside down, like 6, 9; which becomes 9, 6 on turning. The rest don't look like numbers at all upside down: 2,3,4,5,7 just come out as ᄅ,Ɛ,ᵗ,ϛ,⅂.

The year 1961 was remarkable in this respect: if

turned upside down, it still looked the same. (Turn the page upside down and see.)

When will the next year like this occur? The answer is at the back of the book.

59 RUBBING TWO STICKS TOGETHER

This is a way of multiplying numbers using two pieces of wood or cardboard; it is what engineers call a *slide rule*. Right at the back of this book, after the answers, you will see a diagram like this:

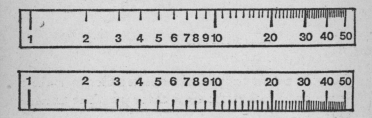

Cut out the numbered strips and stick them on card or wood. (We have put them at the back so that you don't spoil the book when you cut them out.) Make them so that the two marked edges can slide against each other.

You can use these two strips to multiply numbers without knowing the multiplication tables. For instance, suppose you want to multiply 4 by 5. Place the two strips alongside each other, and slide the top strip until the mark '1' on it lies opposite the first number in the problem, 4, on the bottom strip, as shown on the next page.

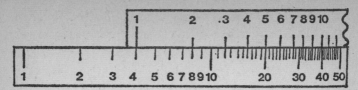

Now look at the *second* figure in the problem, namely 5, in the *top* strip. This lies opposite a figure in the bottom strip ... which? 20, which is the number 4×5 we were looking for. In general, you perform the following actions:

(1) Find the first number in the problem on the *bottom* strip.
(2) Set the '1' in the *top* strip against this.
(3) Find the second number in the *top* strip.
(4) Read off the number in the *bottom* strip opposite it.

This number will be the answer to the multiplication problem.

If your answer is bigger than 50 the method won't work because you go off the end of the scale. There are ways round this; one is to make a longer scale. If you get really interested you can make much more accurate slide rules, or you can buy them for about £1. But don't buy one unless you are *very* interested; the ones you buy are more complicated to use, although based on the same ideas.

60 ANOTHER CRANKSHAFT CODE

'Here's another easy code,' said Professor Crankshaft. 'Suppose you want to send the message "ALL ELE-

PHANTS WEAR GREEN TROUSERS IN THE WINTER". You pick a number, say 8, and write out the message in lines of 8 letters, like this:

```
A L L E L E P H
A N T S W E A R
G R E E N T R O
U S E R S I N T
H E W I N T E R
```

and now write it out using the columns instead of the rows, like this:

AAGUH LNRSE LTEEW ESERI LWNSN EETIT PARNE HROTR.

To decode the message you must count how many letters there are, divide by 8, and write out in groups of that length *downwards*. So if you got the message:

TATD HGTE IEEX SINX MSIX EWNX SRCX SIOX

with 32 letters, you divide 32 by 8, getting 4, and write out the groups of 4 downwards, like this:

```
T H I S M E S S
A G E I S W R I
T T E N I N C O
D E X X X X X X
```

which comes out as "This message is written in code". The Xs are there to fill in the empty spaces.'

Suppose Professor Crankshaft sent you this message:

POLENT ELASTO OISSTN PVSHHE LEHORS
EIOUOX WNULWX HGSDSX

What would it say? You will find the answer at the
back of the book.

61 TANGRAM PARADOX

Both of these Chinese gentlemen can be made out of the
seven *tans* (see page 12); yet one of them seems to have
an extra piece. How can this happen?

You will find the answer at the back of the book.

62 SKELETONS

Here is another skeleton puzzle:

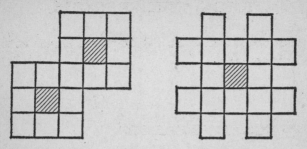

Can you fill in the skeletons with the names of numbers? (See page 23.) You will find the answers at the back of the book.

63 THE BUNGLED SQUARE

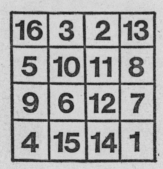

All the lines of four figures in this square, read across or down or diagonally, ought to add up to 34. But by mistake two of them have been placed wrongly. Can you discover which two? The solution is at the back of the book.

$$I \times I = I$$
$$II \times II = I2I$$
$$III \times III = I232I$$
$$IIII \times IIII = I23432I$$
$$IIIII \times IIIII = I2345432I$$
$$IIIIII \times IIIIII = I234565432I$$
$$IIIIIII \times IIIIIII = I23456765432I$$
$$IIIIIIII \times IIIIIIII = I2345678765432I$$
$$IIIIIIIII \times IIIIIIIII = I234567898765432I$$

What happens for IIIIIIIIII × IIIIIIIIII? The answer is at the back of the book.

65 THE KÖNIGSBERG BRIDGES

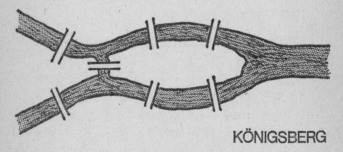

KÖNIGSBERG

This is an old and famous puzzle. This is a map of the town of Kaliningrad (which used to be called Königsberg when people first thought of the puzzle). Can you show the townspeople of Königsberg how to take a Sunday afternoon stroll that visits each of the parts of the town and crosses each bridge over the River Pregel once and once only? The answer is at the back of the book.

This is a very odd maze. The object is not to get to somewhere else, but to get back where you started from, without ever retracing your steps.

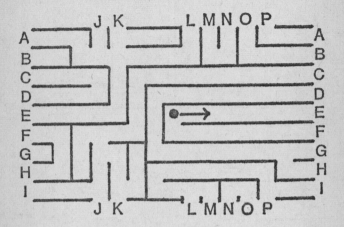

You must leave the centre (marked with a dot) in the direction of the arrow. Whenever a path reaches the edge of the maze you must go to the *opposite* edge, marked by the same letter, and continue from there. For example, at the start you go off on the right-hand side at E; you must carry on on the *left-hand* side still in channel E. Or if you go off the top at K you must continue at the bottom, also at K.

Proceeding like this you must get back to the dot, reaching it from the direction opposite the arrow, that is, along channel F.

The method of shading in dead ends described on page 34 works just as well here, but finding out exactly what is a dead end is rather difficult!

Even Professor Crankshaft's computer behaves strangely at times . . .

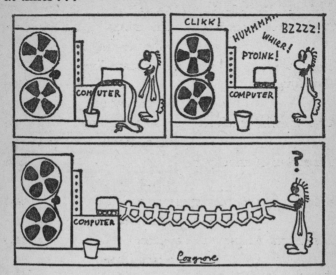

68 SLICING THE DOUGHNUT

Into how many pieces can you cut this ring-shaped doughnut with three straight cuts?

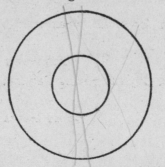

You will find an answer at the back of the book.

Follow this closely:

The number of days in a year is	365	
If you sleep 8 hours a day that makes ..	122	days
which leaves ..	243	
There are 52 weekends, each 2 days long, making	104	days
which leaves ..	139	
One hour for breakfast every morning takes	15	days
which leaves ..	124	
Three weeks' holiday is	21	days
which leaves ..	103	
Four hours free every evening takes up ..	61	days
which leaves ..	42	
Easter and Whitsun take another	2	days
which leaves ..	40	
Two hours' lunch break every day occupies	30	days
which leaves ..	10	
August Bank Holiday removes another ..	1	day
which leaves ..	9	
Half an hour for coffee break every day takes	7	days
which leaves ..	2	
But Christmas Day and Boxing Day take up another	2	days
which leaves ..	0	days

for working.

So nobody works at all!

70 TUMBLER JUMBLER

Try this problem out on your friends. Take three glass tumblers (cups will do, or plastic mugs) and place them in a line like this, with the two outside ones upside down.

Tell your friends to do the following: take any two of the tumblers which are *next to each other* and turn them *both* the other way up. Repeat this until all three are the right way up. This is quite easy, if you turn first the pair 1, 2 and then the pair 2, 3 you've finished. *Now* place the tumblers like this:

with the *middle* one upside down; and tell them to do the same problem. However long they try, they will fail, for *it can't be done*!

For greater effect, you can explain the problem and show them how to do it with the *first* arrangement, and then, without telling them, arrange the tumblers in the impossible position before they try. See how long it takes before they realize what has happened!

71 TAP-AN-ANIMAL

Ask a friend to pick an animal on this diagram, without telling you what it is.

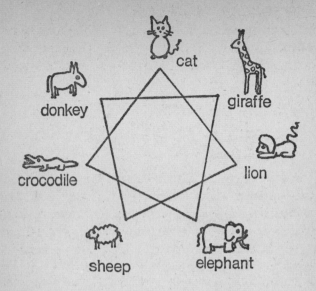

You are going to guess what animal he has chosen. Take a pencil; say that you are going to tap various animals in order, and tell him to spell the name of his animal silently to himself, *one letter for each tap*. When he reaches the last letter tell him to shout 'stop'. The pencil will be resting on the animal he has chosen.

Method: start tapping at the elephant, then the crocodile, cat, lion, sheep, donkey, and so on, following the lines. Whichever animal he chooses the trick will work automatically. For example, suppose he chooses the lion.

As you tap 'elephant' he thinks	.. ..	L
As you tap 'crocodile' he thinks	.. ..	I
As you tap 'cat' he thinks	.. .. ..	O
As you tap 'lion' he thinks	.. .. ..	N

and calls 'stop'. The pencil is resting on the lion.

Get a friend to draw a map of an island divided into counties, like this:

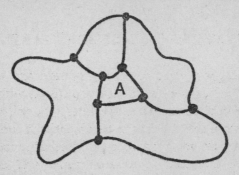

You mustn't look at what he has drawn; yet you will be able to tell him something about his map without ever seeing it!

Ask him to count up the following things:

(1) The number of counties.
(2) The number of points where two or more borders meet – marked in the diagram by dots.
(3) The number of borders – the lines between the dots. Be careful to count a new border every time you come to a dot; in the map above county A has *four* borders.

Now tell him to add up numbers (1) and (2), and take away (3) from the total.

You now tell him the answer.

Method: whatever map he draws, however complicated, the answer is *always* 1. So you say '1', knowing you are bound to be right.

This remarkable property of maps was discovered by an Austrian called Euler; who was also the first person to solve the problem of the Königsberg Bridges (page 76).

73 COVERING THE CHESSBOARD

Have you got a chess or draughts board and a set of dominoes? If so, here is a puzzle you can do with them. Most sets of dominoes have 28 pieces; you will need to cut out three more pieces of cardboard the same size. If you haven't got a board or a set of dominoes, you can make a board on squared paper and cut out cardboard rectangles for dominoes.

Imagine that two corner squares of your chessboard have been removed, so that it looks like this:

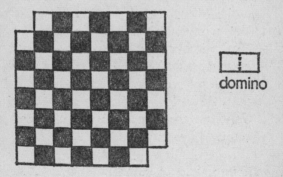

domino

Can you cover this board with 31 dominoes, so that each domino covers two squares? (If you make the dominoes from card, cut them the same size as two squares of the board. Ordinary dominoes are usually a bit smaller than this, but you can lay them on the board across two squares and leave gaps.) You need 31 dominoes because each covers two squares and there are 62 squares on the board when the corners are removed. You can also try this puzzle drawing possible arrangements on squared paper, without using any cardboard.

The answer is at the back of the book.

74 NUMBER PATTERNS

$$9 \times 9 = 81$$
$$99 \times 99 = 9801$$
$$999 \times 999 = 998001$$
$$9999 \times 9999 = 99980001$$
$$99999 \times 99999 = 9999800001$$
$$999999 \times 999999 = 999998000001$$
$$9999999 \times 9999999 = 99999980000001$$
$$99999999 \times 99999999 = 9999999800000001$$
$$999999999 \times 999999999 = 999999998000000001$$

Can you work out $9999999999 \times 9999999999$? The answer is at the back of the book, but you ought to be able to guess.

75 A CODE WHICH DOESN'T USE LETTERS

'On the subject of codes,' said Professor Crankshaft, 'you realize of course that codes can be made using all sorts of shapes and symbols, not just letters. Here's one with circles and plus-signs which is easy to write but hard to decode unless you know how. Each letter of the alphabet has its own series of signs:

A ooooo	B oooo+	C ooo+o
D ooo++	E oo+oo	F oo+o+
G oo++o	H oo+++	I o+ooo
J o+oo+	K o+o+o	L o+o++
M o++oo	N o++o+	O o+++o
P o++++	Q +oooo	R +ooo+
S +oo+o	T +oo++	U +o+oo
V +o+o+	W +o++o	X +o+++
Y ++ooo	Z ++oo+'	

'Like morse code!' we said excitedly.

'A *bit* like morse code,' sniffed the Professor haughtily, 'but much better. Now, to code a message we write the symbols for the letters of each word underneath each other, but the words in order as usual. Suppose we want to code the message "Lunch Time". Write the symbols for L,U,N,C,H under each other, and beside them the symbols for T,I,M,E, like this:

(L)	o+o++	(T)	+oo++
(U)	+o+oo	(I)	o+ooo
(N)	o++o+	(M)	o++oo
(C)	ooo+o	(E)	oo+oo
(H)	oo+++'		

(The letters in brackets are just to give you the idea.)

'You can make it look more complicated by adding extra lines to connect up every + and o, as long as you don't confuse things. Like this:

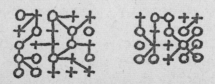

Suppose, then, you wanted to send the code message "I LIKE THE BEATLES". How would it look in o's and +'s? And what does this message (in the more complicated style) mean?'

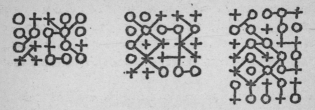

You will find the answers at the end of the book.

This is quite a useful code, because it doesn't *look* like one, it's just lots of little squiggles and things arranged in complicated patterns. Try it out with your friends, sending each other code messages. But don't let the schoolteacher catch you!

It's very easy to invent your own codes. You could use this one with o's and x's instead of o's and +'s, for instance. Or make small changes to other codes given in the book. Use different ways of rearranging the letters. It's great fun, and much nicer if you can use your *own* code. Make up code messages and see if your friends can work out from them what the code is, without being told. Get them to make up codes and see if *you* can work them out.

76 HOW TO MEMORIZE THE TELEPHONE DIRECTORY

To do this trick you have to decide on whom you will try it out. On the day you do the trick, take the day's date, add 2, and multiply by the number of brothers and sisters that the person you intend to try it out on has. Look up the page with the resulting number in the telephone directory, and memorize the seventh name down the page. (For example, your friend has 5 brothers and sisters, and the date is the 13th. You add 2 to 13, getting 15, multiply by 5, and get 75. Memorize the seventh name on page 75. Let us assume it is J. Bloggs.)

Now you are ready to do the trick (don't forget that name!)

Ask your friend to think of a number. Tell him to double it, divide by the number he first thought of, add the day's date and multiply by the number of his brothers and sisters. Tell him to look up the resulting page of the telephone directory, and you will tell him what the seventh name on the page is.

You tell him the name you worked out beforehand (J. Bloggs), to his great amazement.

Don't however, do the trick twice on the same day, or he will rapidly realize just how much of the telephone directory you have *really* memorized!

77 REP-TILES

Cut this shape out 16 times (if you use paper you can do this more quickly by cutting 4 pieces from 4 thicknesses of paper).

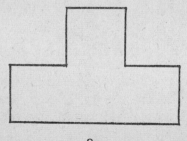

Can you arrange the 16 pieces to make the same shape? It will be 4 times as large. The answer is at the back of the book (one answer; but there *are* other ways).

78 MAKING A HUNDRED

Can you make this sum correct?

$$1 \quad 2 \quad 3 \quad 4 \quad 5 \quad 6 \quad 7 \quad 8 \quad 9 = 100$$

You may insert any arithmetical signs ($+ - \times \div$ and brackets) between the figures on the left.

Answers are at the back of the book.

79 ARRANGING THINGS IN ORDER

The 26 letters of the alphabet are usually arranged in this order:

ABCDEFGHIJKLMNOPQRSTUVWXYZ

But there are lots and lots of other orders in which they could be arranged, like:

BADCXYZEFHGWUVTRSJKILMOPNQ
ADCXYZEFHGWUVTRSJKILMOPNQB

and so on. It is possible to find out exactly how many different ways there are of arranging things without actually working out the arrangements.

One letter can be arranged only one way:

A

Two letters can be arranged in 2 ways:

AB   BA

Three letters can be arranged in 6 ways:

ABC ACB BAC BCA CAB CBA

Four letters can be arranged in 24 ways. Can you write them down?

In general, to find the number of ways of arranging a given number of letters, you multiply together all the numbers 1, 2, 3 ... until you get to the number of letters. The answer to this long-multiplication sum is the number of arrangements. So for 1 letter you work out 1; for 2 letters $1 \times 2 = 2$; for 3 letters $1 \times 2 \times 3 = 6$; for 4 letters $1 \times 2 \times 3 \times 4 = 24$. Ten letters would give $1 \times 2 \times 3 \times 4 \times 5 \times 6 \times 7 \times 8 \times 9 \times 10$ arrangements, which is 3628800. In how many ways can the alphabet be arranged? You will find the answers at the back of the book.

80 HEXAPAWN

This is a game for two players, played with three white and three black pawns from a chess set. If you like, any counters will do as long as they are different colours. The board is a small one:

The pawns move exactly as they do in chess. They may move straight forward, one square at a time, unless they are capturing an enemy piece, when they move diagonally forwards. Like this:

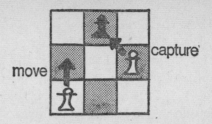

You win a game of Hexapawn by:
(a) reaching the far side of the board with any one of your pieces;
(b) capturing all your opponent's pieces;
(c) getting your opponent into a position where he cannot move.

Here is a position in a game where White loses because there is nowhere to move:

81 A FAMOUS PUZZLE

Each of three houses has to be supplied with water, gas, and electricity. On the opposite page is a map showing the houses and the sources of supply:

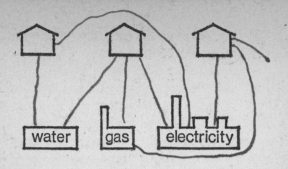

Can you draw lines connecting each of the houses to each of the three services (water, gas, electricity)? The lines must not cross each other or pass through any of the buildings on the map. See the back of the book for the answer.

82 HOW MANY?

How many triangles are there in this picture?

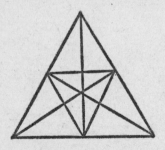

The answer is at the back of the book.

83 CRANKSHAFT ON PARADOXES

'It's funny,' said Professor Crankshaft, 'but people don't seem to believe what I say any more. Why, only the other day I said to the gardener "I am not telling the truth" and he wouldn't believe me.'

'But if you weren't telling the truth,' we put in, 'then you would be lying when you said you weren't telling the truth, so you *would* be telling the truth. And that would mean you *weren't* telling the truth . . .'

'Precisely,' snapped the Professor. 'I began to tell him about a planet I had discovered, which has on it an island, in the middle of which is a lake, in the middle of which is an island, in the middle of which is a lake . . . and so on; yet there is only one island and one lake.'

'No wonder he wouldn't believe you,' we said. 'It's impossible.'

'Nonsense! Imagine a planet, half water, half land, like this:

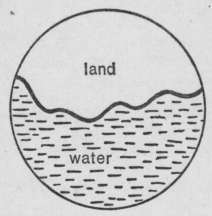

'Then the land is an island in the middle of the water, which forms a lake in the middle of the island . . . and so on.'

Then he started off on another tack:

'I have an animal with ten legs. What is it?'

'Er . . . a *small* centipede?'

'No. It's a dog.'

'Must be a very strange dog!'

'Not at all. Just an ordinary dog. Two forelegs, making eight, and two hindlegs, making ten altogether.'

We said that was cheating.

'Nonsense,' he replied. 'You just have to be careful with language. Which reminds me of the boy who was born in May, and had a *twin* brother born in November . . .'

'Impossible!' we cried.

'Ah, no. May is an island off the coast of Scotland, in the Firth of Forth.'

'Did you say fourth or fifth?'

'Like I said, you have to be careful with language. Which reminds me: what is the longest word in the English language?'

'We know that,' we said excitedly. 'Floccinaucin-ihilipilification, meaning "estimating as worthless" . . .'

'I said, be *careful*! The longest word in "the English language" is the word "language"; the other two words "the" and "English" being shorter . . .'

'But that sort of reasoning would make the first letter of the alphabet be T!'

'Did you say BT? That's not a letter.'

'No. T.'

'Quite right,' said the Professor. 'Just time for a cup. Would you join me?'

'Why, are you coming apart?'

'Kindly leave the funny lines to me. Now, listen carefully. My wife has two heads.'

'We didn't know you were married.'

'I'm not.'

'Then your wife can't have two heads!'

'Oh yes she can. Using your own reasoning, she certainly can't have one head.

'One last question,' said Professor Crankshaft. 'What is the largest district of London?'

'No idea.'

'Wapping.'

84 THE CAT, THE MOUSE, AND THE LUMP OF CHEESE

Professor Crankshaft has been shopping. At the super-market he bought a large lump of cheese. Then he went to the pet shop and bought a cat and a mouse. He is beginning to regret the unfortunate choice of purchases, for this reason: his car is parked on the other side of the road from the pet shop. He cannot leave the cat and mouse alone together in case the cat eats the mouse, nor can he leave the mouse and cheese alone together in case the mouse eats the cheese. He doesn't have to worry about the cat or mouse running away since they are both very tame (and anyway he can shut them in the car or the pet shop).

How can he transfer the cat, the mouse, and the cheese to his car, *carrying only one of them at a time*? The answer is at the back of the book.

85 A MATCHLESS PUZZLE

Here we have 13 matches arranged to make six boxes all the same shape and size:

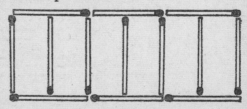

If one of the matches gets broken, so that you have only 12 matches left, can you arrange these 12 matches to enclose six boxes, all the same shape and size? The answer is at the back of the book.

86 A MAZE FOR PEOPLE WHO LIKE MAZES

This is rather large, but quite simple if you use all the

hints about mazes that you have been given. Find your way from the arrow to the dot in the centre,

87 SQUARING THE TRIANGLE

Draw a triangle like this, only larger.

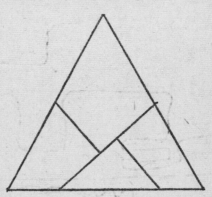

Now, can you cut up this triangle along the lines marked and put the pieces together to form a square?

The answer is at the back of the book.

88 WHAT'S NEXT?

Here is a *'What's Next?'* puzzle without any mathematics! Fill in the next number or letter in each sequence.

(a) O, T, T, F, F, S, S, E. ?
(b) 3, 3, 5, 4, 4, 3, 5, 5. ?
(c) 31, 28, 31, 30, 31, 31. ?
(d) A, E, F, H, I, K, L, ?
(e) 7, 8, 5, 5, 3, 4, 4, 6. ?

The answers are at the back of the book.

89 BAZONKA

To play this game you will need 3 black counters, 3 white counters, and a board like this:

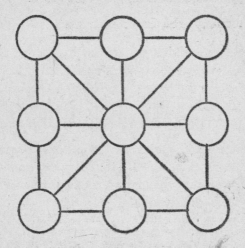

You will also need somebody to play with. You play alternately, putting your pieces in the circles on the board, until all six pieces are down. Then you play alternately, moving your pieces along a line from one circle to the next (in any direction); you may only move one piece each go. The first person to get his three pieces in a line (in any direction) wins. It's like noughts and crosses in a way.

90 SPLITTING FIELD

Farmer Dunk owns a large triangular field, shaped like the drawing on the next page:

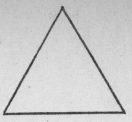

He wishes to divide it between his four sons, so that each of them gets the same shaped piece. How can this be done? See the back of book for the answer.

91 THE DISAPPEARING HOLE

Here are some shapes arranged to form a square. The curious thing about them is that they can be rearranged to form a square that *looks* exactly the same size, but *without the hole in the middle!*

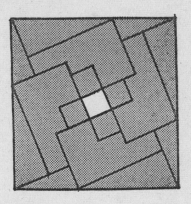

Can you work out how this is done? If you don't mind cutting out complicated shapes, trace the diagram and cut out the pieces. Otherwise try to draw possible ways of rearranging the pieces.

The point about this puzzle is that you would expect

to need an extra piece to fill up the hole, but you don't.
How can this happen?

The answer is at the back of the book.

92 ANOTHER APRIL FOOL QUIZ

(1) How do I put 20 budgerigars in 5 cages so that
there is an odd number of budgerigars in each cage?
(2) Why are coins bearing the name George I very rare?
(3) How many letters are there in the alphabet?
(4) What happens at Christmas Time?
(5) Rearrange the following letters into a well-known
phrase or saying:

AAAEEGHIKLLNNNOOPRRSSWWY

The answers are at the back of the book.

93 CUTTING THE CAKE

If you have a circular cake and a knife, then with
1, 2, 3, or 4 cuts you can divide it into 2, 4, 7, 11 pieces,
as shown:

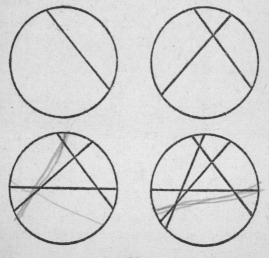

What is the largest number of pieces you can get with 5 straight cuts? See back of book for answer.

94 THE BLINDFOLDED BROOMSTICK TRICK

To find the centre of a broomstick, or some other length of wood or metal, *with your eyes blindfolded*; balance the stick on the edges of your hands, held well apart. Now slide your hands together, towards the centre of the stick. Always keeping it in balance (you will feel the stick heavier on one hand if it is in danger of getting out of balance).

When your hands meet, they will be at the centre of the stick.

(*Can you say the title of this section five times quickly?*)

95 MAGIC STARS

If you add up any of the straight lines of numbers in this 5-pointed star, you always get the same answer, 32.

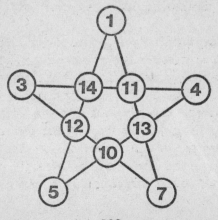

For this 6-pointed star, the total is always 27.

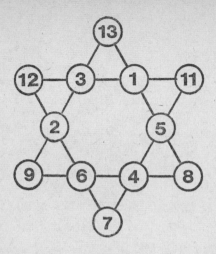

There are more stars like these. Try to find some.

96 THE VILLAGE BARBER

Professor Crankshaft has just come back from his holidays:

'A fascinating little village', he told us, 'very remote indeed: it takes some days of travelling to get to.'

The Professor's usually untidy beard was quite neat and we asked him if he'd had it trimmed.

'Yes indeed,' said the Professor. 'And that was the interesting thing – I was the only bearded man in the village, and the village barber told me that he shaved every man in the village who didn't shave himself.'

'Oh?' we asked curiously. 'Then who shaved the barber?'

Think very carefully and then tell us: who *did* shave the barber? If you give up, you might get some help from the answers at the back of the book.

97 TANGRAMS

Can you arrange the seven *tans* to form this shape? (See page 12.)

You will find the answer at the back of the book.

98 HOW TO DRAW A HEXAGON

You will have noticed lots of hexagons (six-sided figures like the one below) in the pages of this book, and you may have wondered how to draw one. Here is a very simple method using a ruler and a pair of compasses.

Start by drawing a circle. Mark a point on it. Without altering the spacing of the compass, put the compass point on the mark and mark off a new point round the circle. Move the compass to the new point and repeat until you have gone all the way round. Like this:

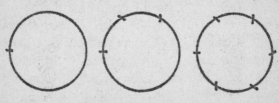

Now join up the marks and you will get a hexagon:

If you draw arcs of circles instead of just small lines you can get this very pretty flower-shape:

99 MAGIC HANDKERCHIEFS

This trick was invented by an American magician called Edwin Tabor. Take two handkerchiefs, one of a dark colour and one of a light colour, and hold them in your left hand as shown in diagram 1. Reach your right hand under the dark handkerchief, hold on to end A, and wrap it once round the other handkerchief (diagram 2).

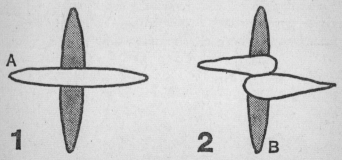

Take end B of the dark handkerchief under and then over the other one (diagram 3). Bring ends B and C together below and hold them in your right hand; bring ends A and D together above and hold them in the left (diagram 4).

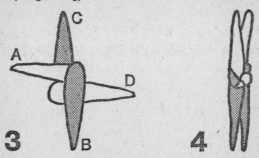

The two handkerchiefs now appear to be knotted together. But it you pull gently, they just fall apart!

If you use large handkerchiefs you can wrap them *twice* round each other (just go over the same steps for a second time, leaving out step 4 until you have repeated 1, 2 and 3). They still come apart when you pull. Try!

100 THE TOWER OF HANOI

There is a very old story about a monastery in Hanoi (in what is now called North Vietnam) where the monks were busily carrying out the following task, which they believed God had set them: on one of three golden spikes lay 64 golden discs; the monks were only allowed to move the discs so that smaller ones were placed upon larger ones, but they were required to transfer the whole pile of 64 discs from one spike to another. They believed that when they had done this, the world would end.

This isn't a difficult task, but as you might have guessed, it takes a long time: even if the monks were very fast workers, it would take them several thousands of millions of years!

This puzzle is a smaller version of the Tower of Hanoi, and is one that you should be able to solve in under a minute. You have FIVE discs (cut them out of cardboard if you can't get gold ones) in decreasing size:

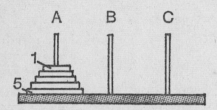

The spikes are not really necessary, and you can just pile up your discs one upon the other.

By always moving a disc on to an empty pile, or on top of a larger disc, can you transfer the whole of the pile of five discs on to another pile – remember you are only allowed to move one disc at a time. The solution is at the back of the book.

2 POSTMAN'S WALK

Here is a map of the town again, this time with the streets widened to show the postman's walk clearly. This walk begins at the Post Office and ends at the village green nearby. There are several possible alternative answers including this one backwards, but all of them have their start and finish at the Post Office and the village green.

3 THE MAGIC HONEYCOMB

Here is one possible answer, but don't be surprised if you found another one. Not all questions have just one answer, and this question has 7,040 possible answers!

1	14	7	12
15	4	9	6
10	5	16	3
8	11	2	13

4 CROSSNUMBER

5 CHOP-STICK

9 THE RIDDLE OF THE SPHINX

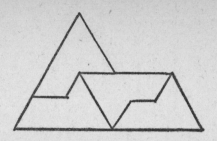

12 WHAT'S NEXT?

(a) 13 (odd numbers); (b) 36 (squares); (c) 64 (double the one before); (d) 22 (differences between consecutive numbers are 1, 2, 3, 4, 5 . . .); (e) 21 (each number is the sum of the two previous numbers).

14 TANGRAMS

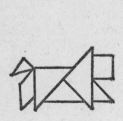

15 SKELETONS

Here is one solution to the skeleton puzzle. There are several more. We give you only one here, so that if you can't think of any at all, you will still be sure that it can be done:

16 FALSEHOODS

Since one statement is true, four of them must be false. So statement number 4 is true. The others are all false.

18 SEAMUS ANDROID

20 MONKEY-PUZZLE

It would take the monkeys about 600,000 years, on average, to type 'DEAR SIR'.

23 SHORTHAND CROSSNUMBER

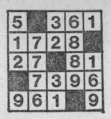

24 REP-TILES

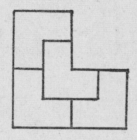

25 NUMBER PATTERNS

6666666666 × 6666666666 = 444444444435555555556

26 CRANKSHAFT THE ILLUSIONIST

The dot and the ring have exactly the same area!

28 PICKING BLACKBERRIES

One way to go down all the lanes once and once only is to follow the dotted path in this diagram:

29 SEAMUS ANDROID

30 HOW MANY?

There are exactly 17 squares. If you didn't get this answer, try counting again and find the ones you missed!

31 STRIP-TEASE

(1) You get a single band with a knot in it.
(2) With four twists you end up with two bands knotted together. With five twists you get one band tied in a very complicated knot.

(3) You get one large band and one small one linked together.

(4) It depends only on the number of twists.

32 CROSSNUMBER

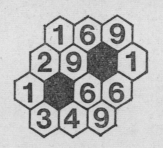

33 MAGIC CIRCLES

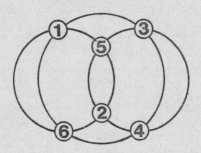

36 REVERSALS

(a) Any of these will do: 12, 23, 34, 45, 56, 67, 78, 89.

(b) 1089. Multiplying by 9 gives 9801, which is 1089 reversed.

(c) 25. $(2 \times 25) + 2 = 52$.

(d) 37. $(2 \times 37) - 1 = 73$.

40 CARDS THAT UNSHUFFLE THEM-SELVES

Use the knitting needle to unshuffle the cards and *then* number them.

41 SKELETONS

There may be more than one solution! Here is *one*:

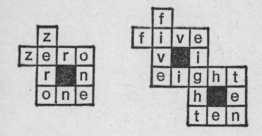

42 CRANKSHAFT ON CODES

The message says:

IF YOU CAN'T DECODE THIS MESSAGE
YOU WILL FIND THE ANSWER AT THE
BACK OF THE BOOK

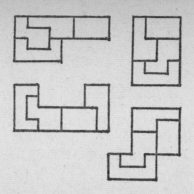

44 NUMBER PATTERNS

7IIIIIIIII7

47 TANGRAMS

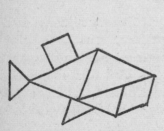 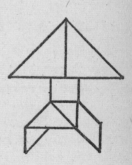

48 WHAT'S NEXT?

(a) 21 (differences are 2, 3, 4, 5, 6 . . .); (b) 38 (differences are the odd numbers 1, 3, 5, 7 . . .); (c) 68 (differences are the numbers in sequence b); (d) 729 (differences are found by doubling the previous number. A simpler way to get the answer is to multiply by 3 each time, though!); (e) 2 (this is a bit of a fraud; it is sequence b) written out backwards).

49 APRIL FOOL QUIZ

(1) 2, one on each side.

(2) All of them. Some have more besides, but they all have 28.

(3) WRONGLY.

(4) 10.

(5) One cat has one tail. But no cat has three tails, so no cat has two more tails than one cat.

(6) The letter R.

(7) 17, every time.

(8) 100 years.

(9) Yes, if I build it at the South pole; where *every* direction is towards the north.

(10) A 50-penny piece and a 5-penny piece. The coin that is *not* the 50-penny piece is the 5-penny piece.

50 GET KNOTTED!

Take the middle of your friend's piece of string; push it away from you under the loop round your right wrist (this may be a tight fit, but it's the only way the trick will work); pass your right hand through the loop you have just formed in your friend's string. If you pull hard now, the string will slip back through the loop round your wrist and you will be free.

52 SEAMUS ANDROID'S VALENTINE

54 A SQUARED RECTANGLE

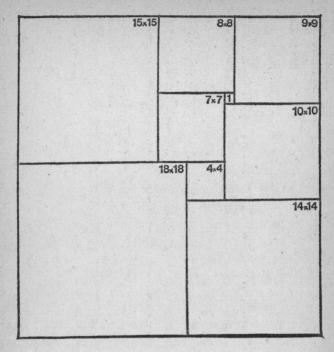

57 REP-TILES

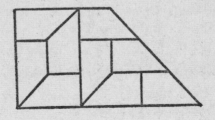

58 TOPSY-TURVY

The year 6009. And after that, 6119, 6699, 6889, 6969.

60 ANOTHER CRANKSHAFT CODE

PEOPLE WHO LIVE IN GLASS HOUSES
SHOULDN'T THROW STONES

61 TANGRAM PARADOX

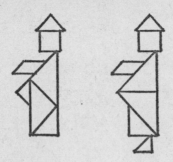

62 SKELETONS

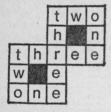   

(there are other possible answers).

63 THE BUNGLED SQUARE

The figures 7 and 12 must be interchanged.

64 NUMBER PATTERNS

IIIIIIIIII × IIIIIIIIII = 123456790087654321.
The pattern breaks down here because of a carry-digit in the middle.

65 THE KÖNIGSBERG BRIDGES

The people of Königsberg cannot take their Sunday walk unless they swim, take a boat, or build another bridge.

68 SLICING THE DOUGHNUT

Nine pieces. Here are two possible ways to cut it:

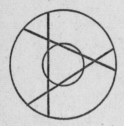 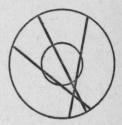

73 COVERING THE CHESSBOARD

No, it's impossible. However you place a domino on the board, it covers one white square and one black. So 31 dominoes cover 31 white squares and 31 black squares. But the board shown has more white squares than black.

74 NUMBER PATTERNS

9999999998oooooooooo1.

75 A CODE WHICH DOESN'T USE LETTERS

'I like the Beatles' comes out as:

o+ooo	o+o++	+oo++	oooo+
	o+ooo	oo+++	oo+oo
	o+o+o	oo+oo	ooooo
	oo+oo		+oo++
			o+o++
			oo+oo
			+oo+o

The coded message reads:

MANY HAPPY RETURNS

77 REP-TILES

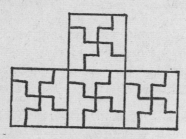

78 MAKING A HUNDRED

There are lots of ways:

$$1+2+3+4+5+6+7+(8\times9) = 100$$
$$-(1\times2)-3-4-5+(6\times7)+(8\times9) = 100$$
$$1+(2\times3)+(4\times5)-6+7+(8\times9) = 100$$
$$(1+2-3-4)\times(5-6-7-8-9) = 100$$
$$1+(2\times3)+4+5+67+8+9 = 100$$
$$(1\times2)+34+56+7-8+9 = 100$$
$$12+3-4+5+67+8+9 = 100$$
$$123-4-5-6-7+8-9 = 100$$
$$123+4-5+67-8-9 = 100$$

$$123 + 45 - 67 + 8 - 9 = 100$$
$$123 - 45 - 67 + 89 = 100$$

79 ARRANGING THINGS IN ORDER

ABCD, ABDC, ACBD, ACDB, ADBC, ADCB,
BACD, BADC, BCAD, BCDA, BDAC, BDCA,
CABD, CADB, CBAD, CBDA, CDAB, CDBA,
DABC, DACB, DBAC, DBCA, DCAB, DCBA.

The alphabet can be arranged in

403291461126605635584000000 ways.

81 A FAMOUS PUZZLE

No! It can't be done.

82 HOW MANY?

Forty-seven. If you got less than this, don't despair – we began with a score of 23 triangles and worked up. If you got more than 47, we won't be surprised, but do check very carefully.

84 THE CAT, THE MOUSE AND THE LUMP OF CHEESE

1. He takes the mouse across and leaves it.
2. He returns empty-handed.
3. He takes the cheese across and leaves it.
4. He brings the mouse back and leaves it.
5. He takes the cat across and leaves it with the cheese.
6. He returns empty-handed.
7. He takes the mouse across.

This isn't the only solution. Another solution in only 7 crossings is exactly the same as this one except that the cat and cheese are interchanged.

85 MATCHLESS PUZZLE

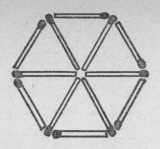

87 SQUARING THE TRIANGLE

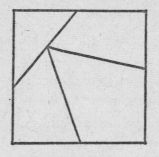

88 WHAT'S NEXT?

(a) E (initial letters of ONE, TWO, THREE ...
etc); (b) 5 (number of letters in ONE, TWO, THREE
... etc); (c) 30 (number of days in January, February
... etc); (d) M (letters in the sequence are those made
up entirely of straight lines); (e) 6 (number of letters
in JANUARY, FEBRUARY ... etc).

90 SPLITTING FIELD

91 THE DISAPPEARING HOLE

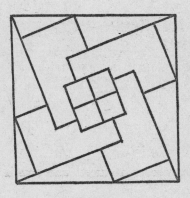

This only works because neither of the figures is really a square: one is slightly fatter at the edges and one slightly thinner.

92 ANOTHER APRIL FOOL QUIZ

(1) One way is to put one budgerigar into each of 4 cages and the remaining 16 into the last cage. Sixteen is a *very* odd number to have in a birdcage!

(2) There aren't any of them! Coins of George Ist's reign would have been marked 'George' without any number.

(3) Eleven. The first is T, the second H, the third E . . . etc.

(4) Christmas.

(5) 'A WELL-KNOWN PHRASE OR SAYING'

93 CUTTING THE CAKE

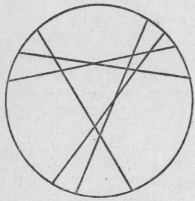

There are 16 pieces at most, and this is one way of getting them.

96 THE VILLAGE BARBER

We think Professor Crankshaft was wrong. There can't be a village in which the barber shaves everyone who doesn't shave himself – unless, of course, the barber is a woman or has a beard (and if you read the piece carefully, you will see that these are both ruled out). You will understand *why* this village can't exist if you reason that: if the barber doesn't shave himself then he is one of the people who is shaved by the barber; if he does shave himself, then he isn't shaved by the barber.

If he does, he doesn't and if he doesn't he does – if you see what we mean!

97 TANGRAMS

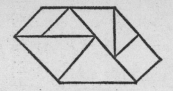

100 THE TOWER OF HANOI

The smallest disc is numbered 1, the next smallest, 2, and so on up to the largest which is 5. If we write '1B' meaning 'move disc 1 to spike (or pile) B', and so on, you can solve the puzzle in the smallest number of moves as follows:

1B, 2C, 1C, 3B, 1A, 2B, 1B, 4C, 1C, 2A, 1A, 3C, 1B, 2C, 1C, 5B, 1A, 2B, 1B, 3A, 1C, 2A, 1A, 4B, 1B, 2C, 1C, 3B, 1A, 2B, 1B.

This moves all the discs from pile A to pile B.

As we said, it takes 64 discs to end the world. Five discs seems about the right size for something much smaller, such as a puzzle book ... so ...